Please return or renew by
latest date below

LOANS MAY BE RENEWED BY PHONE
648-5710

D1531025

Rosentrout by Florence Vale
PHOTO BY WALLY BALLACH

BRIDES
of the
STREAM

JOE ROSENBLATT

oolichan books

LANTZVILLE, BRITISH COLUMBIA, CANADA

1983

Canadian Cataloguing in Publication Data
Rosenblatt, Joe, 1933-

    Brides of the stream
Poems.
ISBN 0-88982-048-1

I. Title.
PS8535.084B7   C811'.54   C83-091261-4
PR9199.3.R59B7

Publication of this book has been financially
assisted by the Canada Council and by the Government
of British Columbia through the British Columbia
Cultural Fund and the British Columbia Lottery Fund.

Published by
OOLICHAN BOOKS
P.O. Box 10
Lantzville, B.C. VOR 2HO

Printed in Canada by
MORRISS PRINTING COMPANY LTD.
Victoria, B.C.

For Faye

I looked for life and saw it was a shade

CHIDIOCK TICHBORNE

Sleep is the interest we have to pay on
the capital which is called in at Death

SCHOPENHAUER
Our Relation to Ourselves

Daughters

I've arrived at a leaf-dead path
to see a bullfrog ride
on a deep brown log . . .
females of the Steelhead tribe
weep for a heavy insomniac
where melody rubs on stone.

Drawing in his lovelies for a harem
a submarine expels a prayer
and they enter thru the portal of his mouth.

My daughters, a ring of gold I give to thee
the sad stars sing under my casual skin.

Blind Date

A few miles along the highway from where I live on Vancouver Island, the Little Qualicum winds under a bridge toward the sea. I approached the river with some apprehension, my first blind date. Would she accept elements of my personality, my 'fraudful' flies? I saw her rejoicing in melting mountain snow and rising winter rain. Pan-sized trout leapt and swam in serpentine rhythm, camouflaged against an amber-pebbled floor. Under the overhanging branches they lapsed into a suspended vigil, periodically bubbling up a hydrological sermon.

I cupped the water, tasting traces of iron, copper, iodine and other metallic essences. A spirit, I conjectured, was trapped in its mineral phase. A dark force was projecting thoughts. Hues of green swirled into the anonymity of shadows where Neptunites dissolved. On that bright day, however, truth displayed a vicious nudity. I peered through a clear window at a brutish member of the Order of the Aquatic Tabernacle. Moving in on a minnow, he turned momentarily to gaze at me. I saw Uncle Nathan's eyes; neutral gray, they looked right through me. My shadow had polluted his lair. His twisted lips mouthed, 'Keep away from my brides.'

The Bride

There is a woman whose song is minnow
a shadow moving out of view: my bride
swimming among dead black branches.
All afternoon I delivered fertile red moons
and when ennui tugged, I offered a nuptial meal:
conversational worms . . . a hypnotic blue fly . . .
This hook caught in a soft frozen mouth
where darkness nibbles at a pebbled floor.

Plat du Jour

Their approach to the margins of the stream corresponds to elemental impressions. They tend to be cautious, assuming each morsel could cause them a little discomfort. Gradually they become accustomed to storing up pleasurable images.

The angler, struggling to decipher the *plat du jour* for pampered felines in troutly clothing, discovers a lusty worm is an answer to gastric mood deviation. Offered in early morning, or late afternoon, trout take to the worm as a weakling would to a virility pill promising a he-man's body in a Palm Springs' tan. A worm, taken liberally, brings out the girth in a spotted pansy. Washed into the stream by an angry rain god, such offerings seldom throw an ominous shade. The meat-filled string of prose is a prophylaxis against a fishless day. Such vision provides magic when I'm out for meat, not musing with a fly. Let them wiggle on their cross, locked into the jaw of the cannibal of my dreams.

The brides prefer a cool summer's luncheon. A speckled heart hastens. The finned ethnicity strikes at *worm mignon*.

Rinsed in speckled silver and gold, they daintily examine each food particle as meticulously as an accountant going over his ledger. In seconds, the Neptunites dissolve. The trout catch a shadow thinner than a grass snake . . . my flyline . . .

The angler feels superior to a trout spooked by a shadow. His artifact, a sacred staff, a promising line of liturgy, competes with Nature's allurement. She has invented the game, and in the process, evened the odds: a warning device installed in her babes, a finicky diet. The brides won't dine on a trophy at length. Vigilant as a rebel who'll not sleep two evenings in a row in the same bed, but roves from one hiding place to another, trout are cognizant that anglers too have read their menu. They reject poetic detritus and other floatable vanities. Trout disappear at the materialization of ink. Unlike the primitive who believes that a shadow is a disconnected soul unable to anchor because of a previous transgression, trout drop those superstitious bubbles. They blow away ethereal ova, empty condominiums . . . promises . . . theories . . .

'I want a beef steak. Give me a real worm,' Nathan mumbles. Trout are always writing aquatic novels. Of course, they're left unfinished.

I flash my Yellow Sally hoping to attract a 'breathing machine' with rose spots running along a medial line. My Sally is naturally ineffectual. I don't have a Zulu. The patent has long expired with the Empire. I sail out one false hors d'oeuvre after another. No chromatic messages sing. No panegyric. I try a Pond Olive. None gorge upon these valuable insects. There's no rapid hungry rush, toward the verticil surfacing . . . Would they accept a Red Palmer . . . Dark Montreal . . . Western Bee . . . Ginger Spider . . . Black Gnat . . . Red Ant . . . Professor . . . Muddler Minnow . . . Teal and Silver . . . ?

You never let me down, honest conquering worm.

Motoring Home

Noon voyeurs present their wounded red gills to a miniaturized whale. He ignores them, beaming on a confused helicopter relaying a distress signal above the meniscus: a frosty dragonfly has run out of fuel. Leaning into the boiling water, the machine explodes, crunched as though the phantom had been there all the while tuning up a crystal musicality. Later, blood shining in his mouth, he slips through a liquid maternity ward with the wreck's directional finder intact, humming tediously in his stomach.

Motoring home, the sub detects a troubled grasshopper paddling frantically on the surface. What incredible sex! First, an aircraft and its pilot, and now the ultimate cuisine: Pegasus. He views the little horse, wings aflutter on a screen. The animal is x-rayed, *red and rare*: a shimmer outlines the choice parts of equine succulence. It'll keep the phantom in the submarine happy for at least an afternoon.

Like one touched by a sick shadow, the swimmer moves away, refusing a line of flies. I've dressed them up for their wedding, expecting one among them to consummate the nuptials with a portly trout. Gleefully, they dance, luring a monstrous groom.

Instantly, I see Uncle Nathan's baleful eyes. The killer having swallowed water spiders, careless grasshoppers, and densities of fly, inhales my treachery. His fins jab nervously. I've never seen him so robust. A marvellous catch, if only I could entreat him.

I toss a pebble. It goes on sailing into eternity.

Rage

Dressed as a trout she eloped
the hook pulled away
when she flopped on shore
bellied over broken rock
snaked like a marriage
hissed to choking water
and plunged into the womb.

A blow vibrates on air.
From a ten o'clock position
I cast away a sad affair.
Whistling over basalt of my mind
the stupid sky returns my fly.

A tiny hook tears at a virgin's lip.
If she could speak.
If she could hate.

Sleep is my invisible bride
I tuck her gently away in my creel.

Sartorial

I reclothe my hook with a worm, the largest and fattest from the compost heap. Now it'll rival any bug dressed as a dandy.

Glow

Mood food works in many guises: worms and minnows flow in a serpentine rhythm, and frenetic flies jive in their broken circles. Hot, tepid, cool . . . impressionistic edibles drift. Louder colors hold against the stream, others fade. In the Fall, the Little Qualicum crowd becomes more discriminating. A summer's intestinal craving for the hairless caterpillar wanes. The tribe searches over the gravelled brain of the river madam. Staring down on a pore in the river, I see a shadow exhaling.

Accept this hors d'oeuvre. I detach my fluttering mind. I let it slide against the current. The glow of serpentine sex is all that I need.

Earth Intestines

A thick grub worm conveys a whole train of meaning.

Pleased

There are sharks cruising about the dark side of a grasshopper: the sweetest corned beef. On cue from a sleeping mystic, zombie trout rise. The Fishing Master has spoken from a suspended position in the river. Hidden away from insulting sunlight they await the first sleepy cicada to vibrate a membrane to others of the gnat persuasion. It intrigues me how many pilots have committed suicide. It is as though a biological clock has suddenly stopped. There are more explosions: Nathan's disciples munch upon their heavenly guests.

From under mossbanks, temporal messages ring to the surface. Proven clean, the brides breathe on their luncheons. Juices stimulated, they are cats stalking their prey, carnivorous, transient ... nibble my shadow.

I find it incomprehensible that a trout compartmentalizes distinctive images the way an evil file clerk files away a political dossier for some future retribution. How dare they reject my impressionistic paintings for those commonplace hyper-realistic clones! I need a smidgin of brain morphine: a psychic mainline ... confidence ...

Gaping Hellmouths gulp down sinners in their thousands. My nerves flicker like deranged water boatmen glued to a skin of water.

Izaak W. A pox on your Palmer Fly!

Poetic Development

Slipping out of your tight-fitting clothes
you pull your legs out of your skin. It's really you.

Dressed in your many-faceted gems
my dragonfly nymph, you've grown stronger.
You've lost weight in the right places
for those spotted lovers in the river.

'Keep away from my overhanging window,'
reverberates a gastronome
reading his future in the pebbles:
there's one final molt.

Out of your skin-tight clothes
no longer a nymph, but a phosphorescent lady
you glide into a grasshopper-crowded summer.

Flesh

I touched flesh with my eyes
It was that of a woman with scales
The lips were thick, and closed
She had swallowed all my symbols

The phantom appeared and winked
I kept hauling it up
The eyes were bluer than mine
She floundered on sand
and the sea gleamed

I pitched my wishes back into the black water

Mother

In the larger sphere we are not far removed from fish.
We are corralled, chosen for some upstream demise. A
dark minnowy presence swims through every pore. In
the Beginning, we gulped down flies like inmates in the
present fishbowls of the criminally insane.

We bubbled in bliss through methane, crunching on
smaller fish. A balanced diet lengthened our girth until
a Voice urged us to try the land. Our eyes blinked,
vestigial hands motioned toward the shore. The food
was plentiful there without a need to play luncheon
host to black and silver diminution. We tore them
apart, webs and all: each human caricature the weight
equivalent of a million flies.

Deep armoured feelings vanished. The Mother un-
dulated below the earth. We cast aside a fishly psyche.

Blue Movie

Silhouettes press against the windows. Evening ob-
longs rove intimately exploring pulses, riffles and cross-
currents. A blue swallow-tail spirals down an invisible
staircase. The lady in blue shakes her hipless middle.
A curious shark follows her rhythms like a sailor at a
sleazy bar. The dance implies: *come on, sailor, try me.*
    Fade out. The scene changes. A grasshopper mate-
rializes. The creature has swung too far over the edge,
toppling into the drink. In seconds the winged racer
disintegrates into a red vapour.
    I'll see you at the Club Top Hat. A green residue
flutters away and the film now concentrates on a pore
in the river. Our shark flicks to the other side of the
stream. There's an infernal logic here to match the
intelligence of any keen flyfisherman: If one grass-
hopper has missed the landing field then there has to
be a hundred who'll take a dive. It is only a matter of
waiting. The shark yawns . . . soothing to have water
rush up against the bruised gums; the Little Qualicum
is an oral hygienist . . . cleaning away corpses . . .
    The shark inhales acres of winged souls. The porno
reel is still humming in his hyperactive brain. His gray
sky fills with a rare intelligence.
    I must write a novel.

Cordon Bleu

Bombardier bugs: they are wonderfully equipped with flanges along their propulsive gland openings in their posterior . . . squirting jets of defensive burning fuel . . . *the flanges direct the flow*

Trout, spoiled dapple bourgeois, needs a constancy of exciting edibles: shrimp turns them on to full heat causing them to breathe quicker, only to dash off for another gastro-intestinal hit, perchance a low moronic aquatic life: flashes in the night . . . again the furious breathing . . . and then there's the case of a drowning mouse . . .

But a libidinous Bombardier bug is a Cordon Bleu snack available only to Nathan, our passionate *shammash*, of the *Temple Bethesda*, in the Little Qualicum.

Secretion

Trout wear a mucous membrane for protection. If the secretion is rubbed away they'll surely perish from some hateful fungus. I'll wear a mucous pysche into the next world.

Sexuality Amongst Aliens

A daylight representative of an evening traveller, a shadow moves quicker through air than a trout through water. Weighed down with its relationship to a full-bodied creature, an indolent outline is dragged to the bottom. Its intensity is deeper than a shadow's lover is dimensional, and because of this neurotic over-kill, the marriage itself falls apart like enriched compost.

Constantly suspicious of shadowy meddlers, our shadow stays close to its mate, ever firm on matters of adhesion: keep away from him (her) . . .

At times in a heat of jealousy the combatants take advantage of the element of surprise. They attack one another to resolve who is the more dominant shade. The result is often a hideous distortion, a sick carbon copy.

I have observed this phenomenon in the interior of a tabernacle in the Little Qualicum: inky oblongs dissolve with no clear winner, leaving a living *spotted fish* perplexed. The trout draws the conclusion that an ego is not nearly as delicious as a fat earth worm. Irritated by a cycle of shady violence, I have seen cutthroat trout assault some emaciated shade more out of boredom than out of contempt. The victim, a residual spirit, has caused an ancient twig to snap in the monster's hyperactive brain. Lipping opaque memory, the macho-submarine motors away to survey other minnowy slivers inhabiting a muscled trout's sphere of influence.

Blind to aqueous elves, shining odds and ends of long-winged succubi in love with trick mirrors in back of their minds, a shadow turns a dark side away from an urgent coition, orgasmic music, blood and spittle. A carbon copy, it is only concerned with self-autonomy. Sexuality amongst aliens is a blemish on the integrity of an embarrassed penumbra at high noon. It must move on in order to feed a compulsion to cling. The shadow finds other game in the stream. A shadow must adhere . . . pebble . . . moth . . . leaf . . .

Silhouettes appear against the windows. They rove over riffles, cross-currents. A shadow brushes against a current, purrs quietly to itself. A ripe grasshopper has toppled into the drink.

A Heart is Armoured
in a Plate of Stone

A heart is armoured in a plate of stone
my creel empty of its little bride
there's no love inside, plump and golden —
some crimson-spotted ingénue . . . reposed.

Restless in their dappled insomnia
brides move like flashes of intuition
silver on silver they slip off their negligees:
a hissing of silk through a storm . . .

An evening glares into my sleepless eyes
those seeds bloom in a sky illumed —
There each terrible moon's a caddis fly
until that neon dies behind the mind:
a dishonoured bride in a diseased motel.

We shall sleep in another's creel
and although there's darkness in the mother
still there's sunshine in her belly.
A voice trickles through a stone that moves:

Do souls have their nimbus then . . .
washed in some catch basin where they grow?
Our bubbling turns to heavy vapour.
There's no haste in this drowsy pool.

Solipsist

'I'm a solipsist,' said my shade
turning the hook;
it was strange
the hook naked
having no worm

I Crave to Swim into a Dream

Swaddled in my gloomy sleep
I crave to swim into a dream
and go on dreaming into stone.

Stones who behold their bride
know each nuptial bed in Heaven,
stones who breathe outside
inhale a minnow from the tribe.

They keep this very silence hidden
only dream that they are drifting
for pebbles sing or go on sleeping
in homage to their hallowed furnace.

Against a drumbeat of the rain
a crowd moves inside to dream —
to view caviar behind the brain.

Buried like a shameful obituary
stones that move and grow . . .

Voyeur's Sonnet

I found myself swimming in a dream
where I disrobed in a spotted bedroom.
There were holes in that quick stream:
each lair offered bed and breakfast.

We cast off our nymphal shuck
those bleeding garments of our faith
to find each nibbling very bright:
an offering inhaled by a somnambulist.

Stir the dark waters, my darker friend
your hieroglyphics fly across the floor
as though they're juveniles fleeing
a trout Beelzebub in residence . . .

Lately, I've learned to dance upon a plate of necromancy
since drowsy crowds have nuzzled into my obituary.

Oral

A shark yawns. There's little else to do but cruise. So much heaven! How much love can a shark take? Silver minnows, their meat sweetened by red ants. It is soothing to have water rush against bruised gums, washing away corpses.

A sky is filled with intelligence. 'Enter my scriptorium, I want to teach you magic words,' Nathan whispers.

Selected Bride

I need no gillie at the stream
to deliver my selected bride
and when she's safely in my net
I'll touch that jellied wedding gown.

Fluttering into a chapel of the sky
a heated fly signals for a bridal kiss
and while lateral fins swim away
the knife of love divides my heart.

Heaven's daughter engages my 'silver doctor'
hooked, she'll be waltzing to my side
I want to be alone with her . . .
and have no others share my jewel.

Rudderless, my senses drift above a pebbled bed.

Caterpillar Dirge

They are small drowning lions
they are tabbies ferocious on a leaf
they are sylphs in golden pyjamas
they are devotees of pleasure
they are adolescents curled up in sleep
they are auditors of all my dreams
they sort out pure from impure thought
they lead us back to the river
they are woollen trains of optimism
they cannot meow 'though they are feline
they surrender and ask for sanctuary
they feel divided
they are souls taking shelter from a storm
they don't want to be moths   Death frightens them
they have taken an oath of silence
they are breaking out soon   Help them
they hate lightbulbs
they avoid cocoons as we hate prisons
they are more female than your mother
they are loved by virile bachelor trout
they are pampered
they are poltergeists in bloom
they are richer than Croesus

they want to be raised on a pedestal
they shun a cat fancier
they are jealous of tabbies
they are loved by children
they have a deep healthy musk
they are not easy to domesticate
they eat far too much mulch
they love warm weather
they fall into rivers
they are not waterproofed
they have emotions 'though they are silent
they have blood
they are loved by spotted fish
they hear the heartbeat of trout
they hear the green blood throb in the leaves
they become barometers of our anxieties
they are small drowning kittens
they are small drowning lions
they are cuddled by children
they are ignored by stray cats
they keep falling into the river
they hear the beat of rain
they understand the darkness

Reflections of Uncle Nathan

Snagged onto a dream, lost in each shadow
souls are minnows jumping through riffles.
I was the glare confused by a spin;
dragged down into the pool like a whisper
I saw others freeze before their *shammash*
for there was Uncle Nathan raised above his dais,
his faith and rock; he was that prayer
billowing a psalm for a cannibal.

These flies apparently seek food above the river, but do not escape the attention of the spotted fishes swimming below. When the fishes observe a fly on the current, they swim stealthily, care not to disturb the currents, lest they should frighten their prey. Coming upward like a shadow, they open their mouths gently, and seize the flies like wolves carrying off sheep from the fold, or eagles take geese from a farmyard; having captured the flies, the fish have nothing to do with such damaged flies, refusing them for their spoiled character.

But fishermen have planned another snare for these spotted fish, and have deceived them with their craftiness. The fisherfolk wrap ruby-colored wool about their hooks, and wind about this wool two feathers, which grow under a cock's wattles and are the color of dark wax.

Fragment from Claudius Aelianus's *De Natura Animalium*, 2nd Century
Flyfishing in Macedonia

Poseur

The classic angling books impart their artificial knowledge, declaring that even in the most fished-out water there is a finned poseur breathing deliciously on your fly like a true erotiphile. Study the waters. What tidbits of peppery creation lie about, what terrestrial has fallen into the drink and is he or she in demand? Any drowning caterpillars struggling ... a grasshopper kicking on that floating mortuary ... a boatman suffering a cardiac arrest ... minnow expired on the surface ... ?

Match your metaphysical hatch ... a brown fly ... a slightly soiled imitation in the sexio-gastro spectrum ... what light is there? ... is your shadow on the water? ... step away from their window, and now cleverly switch the bitch ... do you have a Green Highlander ... Francis Fly ... Dark Montreal ... ?

Trout must write your poem, embrace your precious insect with undulating flanks.

The tug of the sun and moon means little to Nathan honoured in the deepest pools. Does he recall the chatting old hens in the other life laying some bad conversation on him, his soul belching from the inedible confabulation? They spoke of holiness, a good atmosphere in the home, how to prepare a carp. It bored Nathan who brushed away their stale pollen.

Except for one monstrous token carp, there were no other carp in his holding tank. He had the same revulsion to carp that a troutist would to a coarse fish. He cursed his clients for their carpish taste, lecturing them instead on the delicacies of whitefish, trout, pickerel, and even chub; but carp, those sheathed large-scaled monsters, they were the stuff of rude jokes.

I realize that carp is venerated in parts of the world where they are sculptured on bridal beds, cups, columns and boats . . .

In one of my more fertile dreams I had pulled carp, greenishly hued, immensely plated in large scales, huge mouths bubbling obscenities, out of the water. Each time I baited my hook with dough I hooked onto a carp. It went on tediously for hours. The mechanics involved in removing these creatures from the inky deep was stupidly sexual. I was saved by a darker individual who came by in a meatwagon. She needed them for her flytrap garden. Only a carnivorous plant would indulge in tainted meat. Was there a relationship between a bottom feeder and a fly connoisseur?

Carp, away you fertility symbol
feed on maggots of nightmares
& nightsoil wherever it may flow . . .
There is a Nile behind the mind
Trout is for Lovers, & carp for fornication.

'Breathing Machine'
(for Allan Safarik)

I want my fly to dance like Fred Astaire
teasing a trout's chiselled jaw
'til the only sound you hear

melting into the clever air
is the 'breathing machine' of the submarine
I want those feet to pick up the beat

The Princess Emits a Ring of Ecstasy

I'd offer him a lure flashier than any silver dollar he would have stacked away in his antique drawer, but he'd only refuse it. Life taught him to be less acquisitive, to lie back, and wait for a more opportune moment to strike.

My thoughts are dressed in blue flecks and mottled orange. Light as a haiku, they fly toward the nude suburbanite from upstream. He ignores me, switching to a lower fin. I wish I could decipher his vibrating lips. They'd tell where other whispering Nathans glide with their sweet ladies flicking aside curtains of a tabernacle.

It's all lewd and loose in the pools: gyrations, back flips, upward propulsions, obscene encounters, blind thoughtless gropings of a tribal ritual. They touch each other; their movements suggest a continuity of the finned line. Mouthing obscenities, a shadow follows shivering out of their conjugal suites. The witness, Nathan, motors through midnight, a darkness that other swimmers have yet to discover. Distressed by gossip about his double life, he glides cautiously toward the darker side, swallowing a highball.

Another silver drop vibrates on his lips. Pressing lateral fins against his stomach, he induces an ovulation. Memory blooms for Nathan. We are blooming in the same moon.

I see a dying lightbulb in a fish store throwing a jaundiced light on carp, whitefish, pickerel, and trout. Released from a refrigerated dream, freed from ice-crates, they swim in shock. The mist clears revealing a new mother. This is no recovery room, nor is it a maternity ward for mothers expecting minnows. Soon they'll be gutted, fins clipped with a pair of rusty scissors, scales scraped, fine body lines chopped; a filigree of black nerves leap on a butcher's block. Into the sink beneath my skull they slip into the cold water. It invigorates them. The nerves jive. Nathan relishes the black calligraphy, the lettering of his dybbuk . . . a fishy line . . . eternity . . .

Ugly memories are seined through the gill rakes. In his present dilemma he swims around inspecting a prettified fly, an ignited sliver exposing a troubled wispy tail, outstretched legs serving as outriggers loftily supported by gauzy wings: it is a gondola slimmer and more elegant than a tooth deity.

Only his fishmonger's bulk has changed. Pressed into the body of a chiselled stream transient, the terrorist is imbued with a higher animal's cunning. Out of fear for their own safety, water nymphs make honeymoon pacts with the bruiser. They flash Nathan a high sign, betraying a gnat sweeter than the pastrami of a dark moth. The fellow melts into the crowd. There is safety in numbers: zug bugs, muddlers, dizzy hellgrammites and an assortment of other erotic travesties. These form components of a blue movie for Nathan who changes his own reels after every meal.

With a desire to go on devouring, Nathan imagines a princess more richly endowed than a housefly in suggestive poses. She is hugging the surface of a solar heated pool. An annual debut, her stomach is now a reservoir of air. Her love vibrates outward to panting tiger beetles, bushed bees, jumpy boatmen, and for one of His chosen, Nathan. She pulls away her nymphal skin to get on with the striptease.

The princess emits a ring of ecstasy. Nathan has separated her from a globule of water.

We must wear a physical body
& not go naked

Eidolons escape. They rise in their prayer shawls gulping a tonal poem. Surrendering a silver vapor, a fly-eating hunger gnaws away at their bowels. The brides whisper moon moon moon. Judiciously, the gillrakes sort out the juicy portions: drops of rubies, bubbling sticky & weaving black ants release their egos. Securing an ampersand, I hook on the bait of immortality.

Fred and Ginger

I want my fly to dance like Fred
arm in arm with Ginger
I want them swinging in the air
my soul a bouncing top hat
The river is in menses
with little silver lights. . . .

Song

Fish for my mood
with bread and hook
feelings lie deep
roiling beneath

fish for my shade
this decay of leaves
there I'll breathe
on your spidery line

fish for that trout
who laughs in the pool
offer him your tear
to wash down a maggot

fish for my hunger
who lipped a glimmer
from a silver lady
caught on a wing
when her moon was young

A Painted Harlot

They have ignored my poems. On impulse, they flash upon a painted harlot breathing on it, and then apply the brakes at the last split second. They reject my impressionistic paintings. It seems I've provided the offspring of an aquatic pervert with some mild entertainment, something to tone up their musculature.

Whether trout distinguish one fly from another in the sharpest detail is debatable among the piscatory set. There are so many variables, complex mutations, all subject to different cosmic light. How a Dark Montreal appears under the surface to a trout is open to conjecture. A Montrealer is acceptable currency one day and useless the following. Trout are as prone to mood food as cats are. What temptation to offer them . . . eroticism?

We are at the whim of a flytying netherworld. For fun and profit they fashion a line of creations as surely as a Parisian couturier shapes fashion for curvaceous elegance. I whip a wand out to the invisible mobs in full view like a subway exhibitionist exposing his common appendage. Better to be a predacious bird reflecting a terrible darkness upon the water.

Fat Wives

The fish is a fading mariner
with a monsoon in each eye.
He swims through a foam that sings
of fat wives and sex shinier than lures.

He hears the drum beat
from a trout holocaust.
He summons survivors.
His fins stoke the fire.
Thousands of dark eyes haunt my hook.

Strip the Fat Off...

She is gone in an explosion and another bubble forms in its place. Another memory molecule, very warm, a whole bovine in a bubble. Nathan ... Nathan ... she buzzes. Could one so minute ever die?

Mobs, women of the evening, study his gaseous prayer. His tongue is frozen. The fly harem bores him. Fleeting sweet meatlings, each more sanguine than the other. He closes his eyes. The mood menses of the stream rock him to sleep. Somewhere in his sky a fish hole opens. Nathan charges at the fingerlings devouring them and washing out anxieties through his gills.

A shadow inhales my thoughts. They break loose, fluttering against the current, sinking down into a maternal bed closer to that power which devours her children. My eyes close; a tubular flower moves its fine worm-like hairs. There is a verdigris intelligence in this alien.

'Strip the fat off your soul,' a voice cries within. Suddenly, the air has the pungency of a mortician's breath.

'Strip the fat off ... '

Mansions

Aroused in deepest mansions of the night
trout change their skin inside a speckled chamber
before they levitate above the iridescent vapour;
and singing as though it were a lunar highball
my soul absorbs a little ether out in orbit.

A riffle bubbles, 'Isn't every fish a visiting star?'
Afraid, I pour some wicked moonlight down the hatch:
a woman leers back at me from Heaven . . .
Entangled in my net, a daughter of the river shimmies
flouncing in a silver nightgown; she's finally my bride.

Offers

Tonight the stars will be thick as salt over the Little Qualicum, but not nearly as deep as the sawdust on Uncle Nathan's fishstore floor. Under a dyspeptic light, guilty scales glued to his pudgy hands, he desecrates beast after beast. Webbed in a butterfly net they fall under a rhythmic knife and wooden mallet. Bundled into old newspapers, I feel their palpitating anatomies. I hasten home, fling them into a sink of cold water. To my chagrin, the dead jive on the Sabbath: head, heart, lung, spine . . .

In a cerebral sink their eyes haunt my hook.

It flashes on me that Nathan dealt in a form of contraband desire. Like a Mexican Red Leg spider fondling a fly, he menaced each Neptunite, stroking a surrounding intimacy before dispatching the tribe. Exiled anatomies swim through Nathan's air space. Fish from a previous life urge him to link up with their congregation. Offers of endless golden minnows are waved aside as though they were issued from some impure flood.

Speckled Sky

I cast off my larval clothes
I fling them into a dreamy stream:
a useless flag troubles a private trout
whose stars tremble on a speckled sky.

Pulled by filaments of a careful prayer
I sail past his window through the nymphal air
climbing above the billowed voyageur in a pool.

Closed into those fishy lenses
I'm reduced in gladness between fly and apparition:
my voyeur retrieves his trophy from a furnace.

Alone on a platter I'm shimmering in aspic silence
stilled like a gnat lacquered in amber.

The Nervous Breakdown

I cast a red moon from behind an alder, floating it into a pool, my epistle to the dark tribe. I've memorized the shiny pool slicks, one of Nathan's many retreats. The egg whirls about in that same nervous breakdown. Nathan is dolphining nearby. I hear those turbines, propellers, racing pistons ... oxygenation chambers ... exhalation of deadly gases ... traces of ozone ... blood fuels pumping through veins and arteries ...

Arise, go to Nineveh. Proclaim against its wickedness

The spirit is moving through Moby Nathan. His jaw moves in a dislocation of syllables. Fly-Jonahs sleep in his bowels. He'll not cough them up on dry land. His lips twist in anger. Like a completely independent entity, the heart swims away from an unpalatable mood.

Fly-Jonahs flee to their Tarshish.

A Water Boatman

'Give me another variant,' declares the Venus's-flytrap, its tongue searching for a contemporaneous poem: a shrunken housefly. Moving into a tranquility of pebbles, the 'spotted fish', semaphoring lateral fins for more caddis fly hatchings, ignore an incarnation rising on the surface: a neuropathic water spider. Hands compulsively aching, the watery accountant collects fishy teardrops falling daintily like the softest pearls from a diadem.

What I need is a valet of aquatic elegance with a dash of the harlequin to dress up my frail psyche in the other world.

The Dead have Arrived

The dead have arrived to enjoy my improper flies skittering in the sun near 'a nimble-footed teepee of a spider.' On a leaf, cool croupier, he deals libidinous pearls to his gyrating lady. I have selected a momentary fly. It has no true pilot's heart, but lures like a woman of the night. Frothing like poor emissaries at a generous state luncheon, munchkins snap at a few woollen twists, animal hair, assorted fibres glued to a ghoulish hook. My fly is sent out to drown in circles. The false fly, an unmentionable molecule, is lost.

My mind closes like a Venus's-flytrap. Eyes smaller than aquatic flies burn. A delicate white mouth opens. One has to be guarded about gifts from strangers. Nathan seems to be aware that my dry fly is not palatable. Again I coach my fly in expectation of a primitive jaw moving quicker than a grass snake snapping a viridescent straddler. In the distance the fanatic in me glows: I see an oblong pre-man, a proto-Christ gaffed on a treble hook.

Others have taken the lure, easy sex: *a bright fly on a dark day.* I try another hors d'oeuvre. A green gondola dips an engine in the shade. He refuses this phony grasshopper.

Mock Chicken

I have fed them mock chicken, thoroughbred worms, back bacon bits and other gastro-dreams. They have refused all my offerings. I am cursed. I never seem to have the correct fly, that dry haiku. The river withholds her children. Yet once I fooled her with a rubber worm. My line floats further away to where nervous congregationalists hold their meetings. They bubble laughter before scattering into savage roots of dead trees. Hidden away from insulting sunlight, they await the first vibrating epithalamium.

The pebbled floor receives my eyes.

Wooing

Wooing minnows with cannibal eyes
a lambent mind lichened with age
settles on the transit of thought:
'every spotted rogue has his lair
to violate his virgin in a spotted rage'

Select your food, my spirit sings
there's depth enough down in the pool
to lunch at noon on a dizzy Pegasus
and other drowning inmates, winged or unwinged.

Lip to speckled lip, a fluttering shadow
trembles in dissociation: 'procure me a minnow,
allow me to slip up on her blind side.'

Webs

There are webs that hang down in my world. They hang down into dark pools. We are not alone. Moods are like gnats preserved in wood. Into my silence tiny green tree-frogs leap. Their webs press against my skin, cool like fingers of miniature infants. They are pinching my flesh.

Deep inside I hear an annoying orchestration. A bombardier bug is singing a chemical song.

The Dark Side

The dark side boogies across the room
Give me back my skin
I cry out to a spook.
On a floating bed
my shadow divides into minnows.

Disguises

My disguise works. My eyes revolve like a turret. A miniaturized tabby falls into the drink. The surface serves as a lens magnifying every hair of that multi-legged train. Drifting loosely against a pebbled oblivion, frozen, he'll not sprout into some glorious flying tiger. Unaware of a dark stranger approaching, neither will the other cats bloom into mothy flowers. A determined breath, warm and deceptively calm, envelopes the flock. Without even a yawn, they fold into death. Woollen trains of optimism spin. Fate grins at these little dreamers and losers invite their lunacy.

Midnight respires. In the afternoon, aroused by those carpeted delicacies, his shadow liquefies. Undulous in native rhythms, mouth pulsing, the breathing machine is in love again. Elegiac strings dissolve in the bubbling idiocy. A professional hit. The plutocratic worm disrobed, dishonored, not a hair left, nor fleshly molecule for an incarnation. Cleanly devoured, gastrically anonymous in this life and the next.

I'll not fit into his finny mind and body.

A voyeur always outside the circle of an orgy, the lust is in the transfer of erotic images. My brain is always starved for the minnows in a blue movie inside or outside the water. It was pleasant to watch the virginal lions tumbling from a limb. I eclipsed in their demise. My brain is vigilant as a Venus's-flytrap and hotter than a hen leaping for flies. Had the caterpillars matured, they'd have fluttered up to my nocturnal eyes. I engorge on the creatural possibilities of the river. Off to honeysuckle paradise, an endless state funeral of autumnal bumblebees . . . helicopters hover policing the solemn procession. Nearby, a pore of water stirs: a silent gourmand measures his stupid trophy. An inebriate, Mr. Legs, my 'fraudful' blue fly, turns in ecstacy. Nathan ignores those feelings.

It'll be raining shortly.

An Obsession

An animal dwelling entirely in water as opposed to
one living on land, or partially in the air, throws the
mind's flyline into a false cast. Neptunites cling to
the brain's weed bed, nibble away until a gaseous
notion is expelled. Concept fly versus concept fish.

A domestic fly tools into space, as a fish motors into
an opposite sky. Fed by vicious interiors, they attempt
to free themselves from the earth's oppressive gravity.
Suffering the more acute claustrophobia, a fish desires
to fly out of water. Sadly, our Neptunite fails to ascend
to a finned heaven. I'm obsessed with water as a fish
is inspired by sky. I nearly drowned as a youngster.
Green bubbles pressed against me. My body swayed to
bursting worlds. I pressed out of a chrysalis. Buoyant
like a sea onion my suburban body slipped under for a
third time.

Fish drown naturally. I envy their buoyancy. The
medium suits them. Do they become euphoric when
their mouths fill with air? Flying through water, their
bladder filled with oxygen, the tightly plated swimmers
magnify in acres of sleep. I view their dreamy eyes.
Deeply set, they return my gaze. Water is their opiate
. . . crisp cool air . . . an admixture . . . exhilarates . . .

Nathan leisurely drowns, oblivious to Mr. Legs, pulsing one of his many summer legs.

'Moon' whispers Nathan to fallen leaves; spooked stoneflies ooze out of their brown husks, curious unwed damsels and mayflies evicted from their pupal apartments . . . moody, misty, meaty intelligence.

Gathering her landed gentry, the river turns like a garter snake.

I want all your jassids, crickets, antflies . . .

Ignoring a stronger current, Nathan searches for distillations of moon buried in gravel. His carbon copy slips under a patch of water, fins vibrate. He honors his victim, an exotic beetle. Nathan changes into a whisper.

The Drowning

Lump of pride that methane brings
I clung above you drowning
further out than prayer.
Ever kiss a toad after a rainfall?

Let's pour darkness into a deeper well.
Why would she kiss a country toad
resting on some obscure lip?
I should have been an old shoe.

Strange that a straddler who shuns daylight
turns his webs frantically upon a beam.
This brown frog, a drowning lump . . .
clung above you swimming.

Troutly Woman

She fell asleep on my dark bed.
It was the letter 'S' with her troubled eyes.
'Go lead your flames home again to nasturtium,'
I heard raindrops whisper, 'this is your hour.'

It was she with her moons looking in
but that was in another dream motel.
Low on neon, she moaned: 'No, you mustn't . . . '
A shadow shook her gown of laughing moonlight.

Turning like a speckled trout who'd gone to sleep,
she motioned me over to cool in that glow.

Sky

The outbreak of mutation is love. Nuzzling among weed and gravel, snails, shrimp, and minnows pass water spiders moored to their diving bells. Nathan stares greedily at the sky. Breathing deliciously, a finned poseur embraces grains of salt with undulating flanks.

Coitus Interruptus

I'm not as handsome as a trout, nor nearly as talented.
It would take a valium to put me in Nathan's restful
state. He appears to float on air, his fins wave back and
forth, *but all the rest of him is dead.*

Above, the caterpillars snooze on a leaf. They, too,
are frozen in an afternoon's siesta. My thoughts float
up like amoeba restoring some unhealthy tissue in the
body of our world.

Is an artificial fly a poetic transvestite to Nathan?
How he perceives a gaudy fly below the skirt of the
river is speculative, whereas a selective worm shoots a
direct impulse into the brain of a brawny trout unlike
the uneven rhythms of a fly.

A Fly-Jonah is placed on this planet for a trout's
pleasure. Jonah fulfills Nathan's creative bent and to
thwart his creativity is a violation of psychic coitus, an
interruptus with his moon goddess.

He can't resist those mystico-nutrients anymore than
a maggot turning away from an infected carcass.

A Ruined Woman

A voice swims over to my mottled bride,
'Love, I'm floating my White Miller out to you
to snare you on a single hook of matrimony.'
Where a darker fish refuses every nuptial
beneath those lips of *a deep still pool*
the river cries like a ruined woman
for a minnow returning to an early grave.

Amour

'It is the evening of your belly,' the voice cried behind the curtain. The princess, lovelier and more anxious, dissolved in his brain.

And the Lord spoke unto the fish and it vomited out Jonah upon the dry land

If you're diminished in size, a drowning ant in a brackish pool, the Fishing Master will still find you. There's no getting away from His ocular powers. He'll summon a *great fish* to fetch you should you refuse to convey His message.

Tell those green lumps to desist from mounting each other's backs. A tall order. How does a Fly-Jonah approach an amorous bullfrog without being instantly terminated. Your psychic ovipositor is shaking with eggs of anxiety. You set sail on a catalpa leaf turning your wings on His edict. His hit-creature follows. You've become suddenly more pungent than a Green Olive: a specially designed virgin for a girthy gourmand. In contrast, a cannibal's central menu is mundane. What is a minnow compared to articulating black caviare pregnant with a buzzing benediction?

Release my repentant fellow . . . vomit him forth . . .

The miniaturized great fish refuses to respond to any space satellite.

You spotted rogue . . . I say *. . . release . . .* An inner voice rises in light-years. It is lost in the frost, distorted by the curve in space, and plunges into some gopher hole.

There's no power greater than a current of hunger. A benign smile opens an old wound in his stomach. In piranhic rhythm, he reaches his climax, inhales a black speck of infinity. He logs down into a tabernacle, asleep. The voice continues through a field of static consumption into Nathan's dream.

Why do you move among the shadows? Does the future lie there? Vomit him forth . . .

Another Time Zone

My body dwells in another time zone.
Further out than a flyline, I'm invisible
alone, the better half nibbles on an earthworm
where the Fishing Master snares a speckled woman
spinning like a conscience outside a mortuary.

In a foreign stream we cringe 'neath a mossbank.
Stranger, keep your Dark Montreal and Royal Coachman.
I shoo away your cool Zulu and Green Highlander
for soon my body shall be smaller than a microsecond
and that, dear reader, is the meaning of a teardrop.

Music

A silken apocalypse is conceived from a few grains of
porphyry. Oozing from a bloodied chrysalis, the white-
ness bursting with life reveals a prominent eye on each
hind portion of a yellowish brown wing. Moons of
trout eclipse. Carbon copies unable to contain their
curiosity, shadow the dream like speckled detectives.
The strings ring in their bowels, gastro-music, joy. A
polyphemus moth sweeps the air away from Nathan's
clones, a circle of dancing killer minnows.

I ascend in the direction of the salt in my sky.

The Aquatic Novel

Lured by a dark stranger into darker corridors, a goldfish searches desperately for his image. His narcissism is stronger than an urge to bond with a fickle opposite. Unaware of a fellow admiring his resplendent profile, the goldfish executes a final pirouette. The piranha, painfully aware of aesthetics, when matched up with sunshine, ogles a potential quarter pound teardrop. The wee carpish wings flutter, conducting . . .

A fissure opens. Pin, lock and tumbler vanish. The torpedo's lights brighten. Profaned, goldenboy's transparent hands freeze into an obituary. Our piranha changes into a magical shaver. He zips off a set of golden paddlers, pulses into reverse: thoughtfully, he reflects on his surgical triumph. A phantom fin now shines in lieu of an exiled rudder. In shock, the goldfish climbs into a spin, blood spurting from a stump.

Inspired, the surgeon re-ignites, charges. The other stabilizers vanish quicker than a deli counterman shaving off a fine pastrami leaf. Next, the blades wave goodbye on goldenboy's tail, evaporate, Finally it's done, a memorable teardrop sculpted; psychic coitus without interruptus. A spirit glows, encarnalized by a vicious body that only a mother could love. The piranha swims furiously about, his Stygian soul choked in orgasmic rhythm.

Dishonored, the goldfish spirals to the bottom, leaving a thin serpentine trail of regal blood. Nathan in a piranha smiles. He has tied up the loose ends in the final chapter. A meat-eater of a novel.

Bed and Breakfast

Lured into a dream
I disrobe in a spotted livingroom,
stir dark waters, my darker friend
hieroglyphics lurch across the floor
to form their cryptic lines for a menu.

There are holes in that quick stream
where each lair for rent on route
offers bed and breakfast. This morning
I wooed a blue tailed lady.

Thanatophiles

Nathan absorbs a sub-aquatic alphabet as though it were the very musk from his beloved. Ova burst from a gravel bed. Expelling memory through his gill rakes, he muses on those silver thanatophiles flashing away at a final indignity in November.

Why don't they bubble it through their mouths? Isn't prayer enough?

Mineral Phase

From a fertilized thought I enter a mineral phase. I contain comic personalities: my carapace is violet, stomach, titanium and green. Neutral, the compound eyes freeze some trespassing mood. I stare down at a nude water spider, an incarnation of a feverish accountant rowing across my sky.

Never Wear that Body in My Crypt

You should never wear that body
'cause when you shake your skin
my eyes leap at your plutonic gown.
Never wear your body in the stream.

Flashing a speckled blouse for a thrill
you direct a lightbeam on a flicker:
it shakes its crazy legs like a waterboatman.
My thoughts nibble as in rumination,
you'll need a Dark Montreal for your delivery.

Goddess, you should wear another body.
I see you slowly breathing in a thatched motel;
inside an easy creel you're nearly frozen
a silver woman asleep in a terrarium.
Dreamer, stay away from my divinity . . .

She's mine to feast on and I'll turn her over
see how she swims . . . a butterfly aroused . . .
her rudders vibrating into the storm —
you should never wear that body in my crypt
sadly, those fins paddling . . . toward the moon.

Nimbus

Flying on wings of a grasshopper
I enjoy the fires down below.
Do souls have their protective nimbus then
when hurtling through great speckled matter?

A trout is a voyeur gleaming, an angler.
It is we who are drowning.

We've escaped our unpleasant bodies
and now we find ourselves imprisoned
in a scaly prayershawl, finally exposed:
an iridescence from somebody else's dream.

Conveyed on the wings of a blazing thoroughbred,
I indulge a pod of spotted fish leaping
from a troubled sleep, at noon.

Swing

I offer the brides in the pool a thick black beetle. The meal is on me. They assault it cleverly. Again I hear their laughter. Darkened by a shadow, they ogle a rotating celestial body.

A floral lady shivers in Nathan. 'I need you,' Nathan declares behind the gill rakes. He yearns to swing with Fred and Ginger.

> Rev those engines, pump those pectorals
> 'cause we're all due at the Club Top Hat.
> Let's have some moons, flash those lights
> It's dark down here . . .

A Tapered Green Gowned Lady

A tapered green gowned lady
swims in my fevered brain,
freezes a sad and heavy song:

Choose a bride and flutter
where salt shines on your bed
flow into a solitary minnow.

A tapered green gowned lady
burns in a rosy firmament
and the river renews a pearl

A Shameless Bed

Releasing a desperate brood upon a shameless bed
the brides move slowly down the aisle as in a dream
scattering those treasured pearls among the dead.
This river is a floating mortuary where they lean.

My thoughts are swept beneath each angry bubble,
that gloom suffused inside a tonal poem.
I extend a pelvic fin in my sleep to those in trouble
who slip out to an alabaster kingdom all alone.

Sleep is our mistress enclosed beneath a mucous membrane
fleeing the devouring rhythm along a moving mortuary
where space is mother to a spinning leviathan . . .
In the night those lips surrender a frozen miserere
to final vapours which dissolve a careless cavity
taming the bully flaring at a pregnant void.

Popular Song

Come dance with me, minnow-child
you're slipping further and further away
flashing in the moonlight with a stranger
you shimmy into my dream lipping a song
and I glow 'cause I'm a ghost for you,
babe, do you think we'll ever touch bottom?

Slipping away, I spook the speckled crowd.
Trembling in the deeper manses of the night
they're jiving on top of the landing.
Bubbling away, Love, I'm slipping . . .
laughing 'til all my sandcastles crumble.
Glued to a pearl along the avenue
I turn on a globe, and every star is a fish
that's loving you, silver woman.

Minnow Child

They seek out their father's haunting eyes
each bride, a minnow child, adjusts her speed
to view a slender bridesmaid on the rise.
The angry epicures charge at her chemise . . .

I draw in my spirit to tie on a poltergeist.
Reflecting on Uncle Nathan, stooped and small,
who solemnly brothel'd a serious Neptunarium
I hear a heartbeat racing out in Heaven.

Caterpillar Disarmed

they are fuzzy dreams in dream pajamas
they tease trout through radio signals
they suffer from a dual personality
they have buried angst   don't indulge them
they embrace the female principle
they are found delicious by blind finches
they loom into your life
they are three-dimensional women
they want to be raised on a pedestal
they are jealous of tabbies
they are primitives among the power elite
gold is alien to them

they don't want to drown
they are born blind
they are not easy to domesticate
they eat far too much mulch
they love the warm weather
they take shelter in the storm
they hate the rain on their fur
they are mortal
they have a short time on earth
they are a hedonist pod on a leaf
they resist the temptation to fly
they have met Uncle Nathan in a tabernacle
they serve as bread for his brides

Sunset

Nurtured by a serpent mother
I snake away, breathing heavy water
pursuing those darkest minnows
washed by a winter's spill.

Vibrating, everything on hold,
the self decays, abandoned
to an abstract maggot dreaming snow.
I change into another swimsuit.

Friend, I'm that sunset in your net
when your body's gone upriver.

Morpheus

Dowdy toad walks over the lawn and catches a cricket
rejoicing as those delicious wings unhinge for him:
parochial sounds issue from vibrative musician; ignited-
machineries of love hum a steady anthem . . .

I, too, have hopped their absurd greensward
tho' no mesmerist played a melody for me —
in Mercy, Morpheus laid metal on my lids; restored
my spirit turned toward a palm tree by the angry sea.

I could have been a sunlit finger on a rock
gold for plutocrats of toad gaping at wormy greed
or luring a hermit crab out for his morning walk;
— and domicile abandoned, my urge sidled in the lead.

Carnal toads, forget terrestrial desire and inflamed ambition
'else you'll wear his webs without asbestos, in perdition.

Family

Take your seed elsewhere, Nathan pleads, frightened
by contamination. *Away with you,* Nathan shudders.
Washed out of a uterus, a red moon whirls about a
nervous breakdown. His heart beats faster.
   This is not my son.

They return to the source
their bones filled out with flesh.
Out there on the rim of the world
I see Nathan ascend to his Maker
from the lips of that pool.